The Liminal, The Essential, The Overlooked

Maura Chapman

BookLeaf
Publishing

India | USA | UK

Presentation by *BookLeaf Publishing*

Web: www.bookleafpub.com

E-mail: info@bookleafpub.com

ISBN: 9789357215503

First edition 2022

ACKNOWLEDGEMENT

I would like to thank the unrecognized for helping me choose to pursue this work.

PREFACE

This book contains twenty-one poems embarking on a journey to express the importance of subjects we often forget to acknowledge - subjects that serve as the bedrock for meaning in our existence.

The Bauble Shelf

You embodiment of all that is ironic,
With only displeasure to bring the sullied, unremembering eye,
Yet joy to the nostalgic though even they have no shining pupil to give,
Only an iris whose peripheral cherishes you in the fleeting silent moments,
A clarity and meaning filling the sound, the air, the light between you.

Oh, to box you up and take you away,
To make your competition of dust veils swell with vigor,
And keep you stuffed beneath the sweaty thumb of aesthetic candor!

But hide you away from the golden-brown window,
And fill her with nothingness in the silent moments' passings-by,
And suddenly the recess feels emptier,
Suddenly life seems fuzzier,
Blurry and generic with no vivid lines or remarkable features,
A mirage,
Even in the oasis.

Lightest Green

Delicate, wonderful, lightest green,
How much of a debt I owe to thee.
Your peek in the springtime,
And dance on the leaves,
Your touches on rubies,
And whispers on wings,
In winter, a glory,
In summer, a king.

The Arch

What is it about you?
Why do I make the effort to pass beneath you
each day?
You flank me,
Outdo me,
Watch me,
And swallow me.

I stand here now,
And peer up at you.
I see your smooth curves,
Your cover,
Your protection,
Your steadfast spirit.

Perhaps you remind me of something greater,
Something above me.
That which I long to know,
Yet which will blissfully
　　　　evade me
　　　　　　forever.

Lamentation of a Poetic Fool

I am an adequate writer and nothing more.
I lack the spirit and color to tell the way the
summer breeze tells.

There are many who taste the language of the
blossom,
And face the fields below to let it drip from their
fingers.

Why am I one without color?
Without the language to grow beauty beneath
my own feet?

They say my color was taken away,
A flow of honey drew it far, they say.

But how can this be?
I saw no sea of sweet.
My feet have not left this place.
Neither rock nor storm has moved them.

I look above in hopes of birds,
Answers they might give to me,
But only an empty sky is sweeping.

The sky is blue,
For blue is an idea,
And nothing more.

What's It Like To Grow Up Without The Stars?

What's it like to grow up without the stars?
To not know the jewels in heaven's bow,
And settle for man's faux glimmers?

What's it like to cast eyes ahead and below,
To bend necks 'til defeated they droop,
And shrivel in earth's dense cloak?

Window Pane

Cold
And firm
Warm
And rigid

A single
Spark
Stretched out
Clean

The sand
Pressed
Fire eaten
Blown

At once
One
And yet
Two others.

Eyes Like Others

Whose are these?
I see them.

They are not mine,
They're others.

Looking through,
All is altered.

Needle through thread,
Thread through paper.

Taut but unfamiliar,
Useful only now,
Not later.

These eyes,
They're mine.

There are no others.

Holly

Bind up the staircase,
In fresh nutmeg air,
Where ginger men tiptoe,
In crystal snow fair,

'Round trees that shimmer,
Candle-filled branches,
Where flames play samba,
In amber dances.

How can we repay,
The splash of red-green,
That soars all around us:
A holy day's seam!

Grass On Me

Can it be said,
That I'd be the same,
When my rush down the hill,
My leap in the creek,
My climb up the tree,
My wrestle in leaves,
Surfaced nothing?

What, then, of these harmless blades,
Each clinging to me?

A last chance at life,
Or so it seems.

Collection

Number the pebble,
The stamp,
The gem,
The caps,
And the petals,
The ribbons,
The pens.

And when you are lifted,
Then next when you're lowered,
Find all these things emptied,
Hollow,
Unnumbered.

A Gamble

Tables smoothened
And sanded.

Glasses
Shaded, darkened.

No background.
Just smoke.
A bulb hanging low.

Only stares and games.

What is beneath you,
Little thing,
There on the table?

What do you cover,
What is it you hide?

You decorate your shell,
Weaves and laces,
Fingers and faces,
But none can see through your web.

We wait patiently.

Do turn,
And tuck away your pattern.
Your façade of mystery.

The Whisper

Speak to me, darling,
In a voice soft and low,
Let no one else listen.
Just you and I alone.

The Cold Inside

My skin is like wax,
All melting with fire,
And the sun threatens to invade me.
Heat tears my torso,
While flames pierce my face.

How am I spared?
Not the water drops on my tongue,
Nor the cool cup in my hand.
It's the wintry slide down my body,
The inside,
That brings me a vivacious sensation.

The Frame

She keeps you there,
She bears you up,
Night upon night.

She never gives way,
Or takes one rest,
She persists all the more.

Perhaps she groans,
But give her grace,
If only for your dependence upon her.

Our Tools

Those before us,
Before them,
Before many,
Tested,
Tried,
Taught,
All for function,
For living,
For might.

Give thanks.
Give wonder.

PleaScent

Fortunate you,
And fortunate me,
That when I walk,
We may get on pleasantly.

Our nostrils unbothered,
Our stomachs all sound,
"This time is a wonder!"
We should all resound!

Winter Fade

White rests,
Across the horizon,
From here to there,
Above and below.

But here there are no fluffy flakes.
No freeze,
No ice,
Not even ice skates.

The dullness bears silence.
Unfelt, heavy space.

Their Space

Those two,
So famed.

See them,
Still,
Man on left,
Divine on right.

The man,
He looks,
But reaches,
He doesn't.

The Divine,
He stretches,
Wise,
Aged.

What sits between them?
Can anyone say?
No seraph, no cherub,
Not painter himself.

Not even eyes,
Should they speak,
Could tell.

To never know,
I know.

Look Up

See the zenith.
Focus.
Don't waver.
Keep face in hands.
Don't shiver.
Nothing below is worth your glance.
Please trust me,
I beg,
Look up.

Sole

Shoulder me heavy on your frame,
And carry me far over the rocks,
The hills,
The mountains,
The plains.
Leave me never speared,
Or stabbed,
Or scraped.
To you I smile,
So faintly,
Like the woman surrounded by glass,
A warmth and a thanks.

Do You Wish Them Well?

When your goodbye,
Leaves your lips,
Does your bye mean good?
Depart from here,
And in your heart,
Leave a tiny box.
Wrap it in goodness,
And fold it in sincerity,
Bind it with joy,
And touch it with love.
Do bid a good farewell.